I'M Tired

and Other Body Feelings

Clare Hibbert
Illustrated by Simona Dimitri

amicus

This title has been published with the co-operation of Cherrytree Books
Amicus Illustrated is published by Amicus
P.O. Box 1329, Mankato, Minnesota 56002

Printed in Mankato, Minnesota, USA by CG Book Printers, a division of
Corporate Graphics

Library of Congress Cataloging-in-Publication Data

Hibbert, Clare, 1970-
I'm tired and other body feelings / Clare Hibbert ; illustrated by Simona Dimitri.
p. cm. – (Feelings)
Includes index.
ISBN 978-1-60753-175-3 (library binding)
1. Emotions in children--Juvenile literature. 2. Fatigue--Juvenile literature. I.
Dimitri, Simona. II. Title.
BF723.E6H54 2011
152.4--dc22
2011002235

13-digit ISBN: 978-1-60753-175-3 First Edition 1110987654321
First published in 2010 by Evans Brothers Ltd.
2A Portman Mansions, Chiltern Street, London W1U 6NR, United Kingdom

CONTENTS

Tired

s-t-r-e-t-c-h

yawn

tired

hungry

thirsty

full

4

5

Hungry

We went on a long walk. Then I felt **hungry**.

rumble, rumble

6

tired

hungry

thirsty

full

sick   dizzy   cold   itchy   sore

Thirsty

tired   hungry   thirsty   full

I imagined living in a desert. I felt **thirsty**!

Jingle, jangle

sick

dizzy

cold

itchy

sore

9

sick   dizzy   cold   itchy   sore

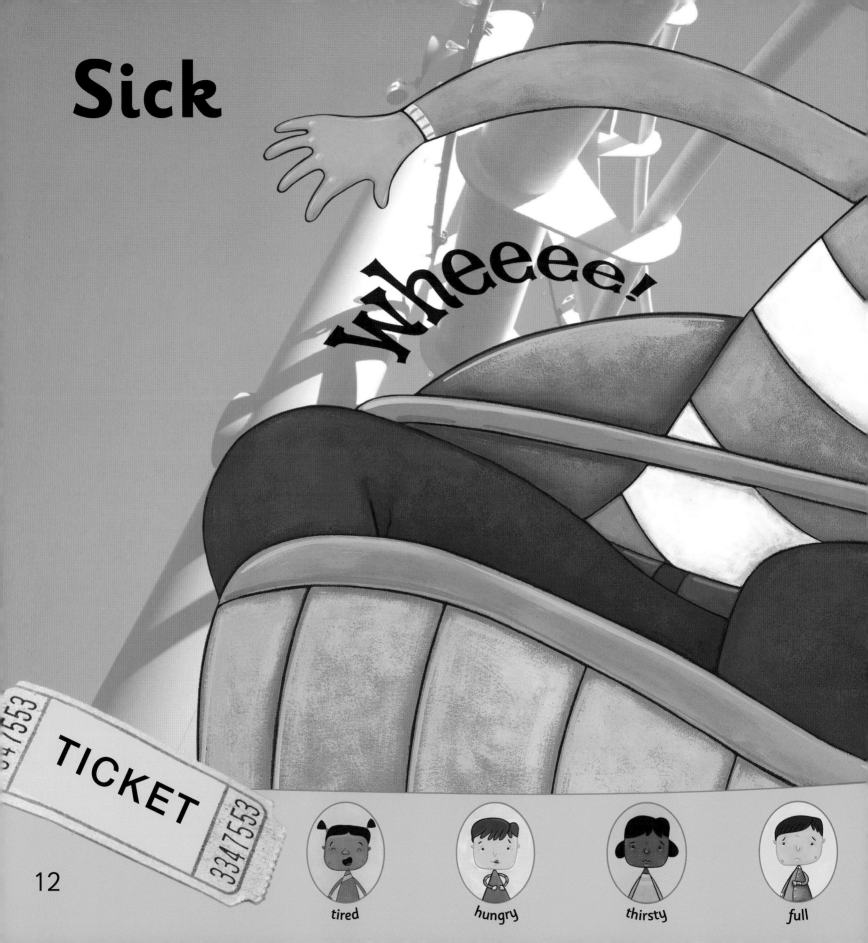

Sick

Wheeee!

TICKET

12

sick dizzy cold itchy sore

13

Dizzy

Whoosh!

14

tired   hungry   thirsty   full

I went on the merry-go-round. I felt **dizzy**.

Whooooh!

sick

dizzy

cold

itchy

sore

brrr!

sick

dizzy

cold

itchy

sore

Itchy

brrmm, brrmm

18

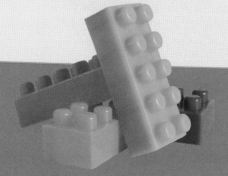

tired

hungry

thirsty

full

19

Sore

I woke up after my operation. My throat felt **sore**.

Croak, croak!

tired | hungry | thirsty | full

20

sick   dizzy   cold   itchy   sore

Notes for Adults

The **Feelings** series has been designed to support and extend the learning of young children. The books tie in with teaching strategies for reading with children. Find out more from the International Reading Association (www.reading.org), and The National Association for the education of Young Children (www.naeyc.org).

The **Feelings** series helps to develop children's knowledge, understanding, and skills in key social and emotional aspects of learning, in particular empathy, self-awareness, and social skills. It aims to help children understand, articulate, and manage their feelings..

Titles in the series:

I'm Happy and Other Fun Feelings looks at positive emotions
I'm Sad and Other Tricky Feelings looks at uncomfortable emotions
I'm Tired and Other Body Feelings looks at physical feelings
I'm Busy a Feelings Story explores other familiar feelings

The **Feelings** books offer the following special features:

1) **matching game**
   a border of faces gives readers the chance to search for the face that matches the sensation covered on the spread;
2) **fantasy scenes**
   since children often explore emotion through stories, dreams and their imaginations, two emotions (in this book, "thirsty" and "cold") are presented in a fantasy setting, giving the opportunity to examine intense feelings in the safety of an unreal context.

Making the most of reading time
When reading with younger children, take time to explore the pictures together. Ask children to find, identify, count or describe different objects. Point out colors and textures. Pause in your reading so that children can ask questions, repeat your words or even predict the next word. This sort of participation develops early reading skills.

Follow the words with your finger as you read. The main text is in Infant Sassoon, a clear, friendly font designed for children learning to read and write. The thought and speech bubbles and sound effects add fun and give the opportunity to distinguish between levels of communication.

Extend children's learning by using this book as a springboard for discussion and follow-up activities. Here are a few ideas:

Pages 4–5: Tired

Do the children know the story of the "Princess and the Pea"? Provide old magazines so that each child can make her a patterned "mattress," then assemble a super-tall mural of the princess's bed. Don't forget to put in the pea and the princess! You could also find pictures of different kinds of beds, such as a bassinet, crib, bunk beds, hammock, four-poster, and futon, then see how many the children can name. Use Internet or museum resources to find images of beds used long ago.

Pages 6–7: Hungry

Encourage children to keep a pictorial food diary for a week. The children can draw what they eat for breakfast, lunch, dinner, and snack times each day. Older children might enjoy being given blank clock faces to stick into their diaries — they can add clock hands to record what time they ate each meal.

Pages 8–9: Thirsty

Help the children to make thirst-quenching fruity cocktails. Allow them to carefully pour some apple juice into the bottom of a tall plastic glass, add slices of fresh fruit, and then top up with water or reduced-sugar lemonade. For the finishing touch, they can add a couple of bendy straws or cocktail umbrellas (be careful — the sticks are sharp).

Pages 10–11: Full

Play-act running a restaurant. Help the children design simple picture menus of the food and drinks, and practice laying tables with tablecloths, napkins and silverware. Children can take turns being aproned restaurant staff or dressed-up diners.

Pages 12–13: Sick

If the children have ever visited a carnival or theme park, ask them to think of different words that express the sensations they felt. Did they prefer fast rides or slow ones? Can they draw or paint pictures of themselves having fun at the fair? Write on sound effects, such as "Whoosh!" and "Wheeee!".

Pages 14–15: Dizzy

Ask the children to draw a map of their local playground. Where are the swings, the merry-go-round, and the slide? What other things are there? What do they like best?

Pages 16–17: Cold

Create a 'cold' collage of Arctic animals. Draw thick outlines first, then stick on screwed-up tissue-paper balls to fill in the shapes: white for polar bears, icebergs, and snowflakes, gray for seals, and blue for any expanses of ocean water.

Pages 18–19: Itchy

The brothers in this picture have chicken pox. Have the children ever had chicken pox, and can they remember how it felt? Ask them to design a get-well card for a friend who's not well.

Pages 20–21: Sore

Think about ways children could pass the time while recovering in the hospital from an operation. Gentle activities can take their mind off feeling sore or uncomfortable. The memory game is a great quiet game. Put ten familiar objects on a tray. While the players close their eyes, take away one object. Who will be first to guess which object is missing?

Index

Credits

The publisher would like to thank the following for permission to reproduce their images:
iStockphoto: cover and 4–5 (scorpion56), 6–7 (AVTG), 6 (slacroix), 8–9 (BremecR), 8bl (muratsen), 8c (Petershort), 8tr (enot-poloskun), 10–11 (manley099), 10 (borisyankov), 12–13 (P_Wei), 12 (davidp), 14–15 (DanBrandenburg), 14 (VMJones), 16–17 (skhoward), 16 (drnadig), 17 (zeremski), 18–19 (vicnt), 18 (carlosalvarez), 20 (belknap);
Shutterstock Images: 4 (photomak), 20–21 (wxin).